EDVARD MUNCH

E.Munch

by Jean Selz

CROWN PUBLISHERS, INC. - NEW YORK

Title page: SELF-PORTRAIT, 1886
Oil, 13¾" × 10"
Collection National Gallery, Oslo

Translated from the French by:

EILEEN B. HENNESSY

LIBRARY OF CONGRESS CATALOG CARD NUMBER: 74-76242 ISBN: 0-517-515717
PRINTED IN ITALY. © 1974 PALLAS SCRIPT AGENCY, S.A. NAEFELS, SWITZERLAND
ALL RIGHTS FOR REPRODUCTION OF PHOTOGRAPHY RESERVED BY MUNCH MUSEET, OSLO
ALL RIGHTS IN THE U.S.A. RESERVED BY CROWN PUBLISHERS, INC., NEW YORK, N.Y.

SPRING, 1889   Oil, 70⅜″ × 110″   Collection National Gallery, Oslo

To Aude Fonquernie

The proto-Expressionists

The practice of referring to the Norwegian painter Edvard Munch (born at Loeten on December 12, 1863; died at Ekely, near Oslo, on January 23, 1944) as either a precursor or one of the most typical representatives of Expressionism has encouraged the continued existence of several misunderstandings. In countries like France and England, whose knowledge of the movement was belated and superficial, one such misunderstanding surrounds the movement defined by this name in Germany. In the latter country it is a movement based in part on national sociological viewpoints, with a Nordic extension; in the former, in contrast, only its aesthetic aspect has been retained. Another misunderstanding has sprung up around the subject of Munch himself: although his Expressionist paintings are his best-known works, a major portion of his work lies

5

completely outside this classification. This book is an attempt to shed some light on the confusion that still surrounds these questions.

As in the case of Impressionism (exclusive of its revolutionary technique, however), it is possible to see in Expressionism, on the one hand, an aesthetic characteristic that is not restricted to any one period, and on the other, a movement consisting of a small number of artists and existing within a clearly delimited period. Awareness of Expressionism has been complicated and made uncertain by the fact that this aesthetic characteristic, which (from our point of view) can be found in a certain number of painters, is not the only one on which the artists in the German movement based their work.

So true is this that the European Expressionist Exhibition, organized by and first shown at the Munich Haus der Kunst, and subsequently shown in 1970 at the Musée National d'Art Moderne in Paris (like the 1974 Edvard Munch Exhibition, which also traveled from Munich to Paris), inevitably startled its French visitors, who were disconcerted to see paintings that in no way corresponded to their idea of Expressionism: abstract pictures by Kandinsky, for example, and works by Klee, Macke, Gauguin (as a precursor of Expressionism), Mondrian, and Pascin.

It is easier, according to our conception, to define the attitude and the aesthetic system of the Expressionist painter than to explain why so many artists, novelists, poets, and dramatists have been included under this single heading. It would be helpful, then, to more closely define the nature of this painting, so that we may understand to what extent Edvard Munch is a part of it.

In its most obvious style of representation, Expressionist painting is lyric and dramatic. It tends to stretch human emotions, and in particular the emotions of sorrow and anxiety, to a point of pronounced tension. It is a style of painting that captures the sadness, unhappiness, and fear that imprison humanity, and thus it is first and foremost a drama in which attention is concentrated on the message communicated to us by the characters. Pure landscapes may also be called «Expressionist,» but only when the character conferred upon them is able to endow them with an expression suggesting or revealing a human emotion.

Let us immediately consider an example of Munch's work that is typically representative of Expressionism: the painting entitled _The Scream_ (see page 29), the very title of which seems to summarize all the definitions applicable to this style of painting. By analogy with the expression of thought, we could say that the Expressionist style cannot be satisfied with speech, still less with a murmur; it requires that action by which the human being liberates himself from an emotional impulse that originates in a source more instinctive and less easily analyzed than thought, and which stands outside the logic of spoken language: shouting. In Munch's painting, the cry dominates the composition and imposes itself directly upon our vision by the almost central position in the foreground occupied by the open mouth of the figure holding its head in its hands. The person uttering it is walking along a road that disappears into the distance, and his back is turned to a landscape in which an expanse of dark blue water contrasts with the red bands streaking across a yellow sky. The cry uttered by this person in the grip of an unknown terror would not produce such a powerful impression upon us were it not for the way in which the painter has been able to suggest, by using the technique applied in depicting the landscape, the inner agitations that impart to this cry its powerful motivation. The entire landscape beyond the railing appears in a movement of sinuous lines in which the trails of paint, with their soft and indecisive shapes, are as it were an

6

MORNING, 1884   Oil, 40¼″ × 43⅛″   Collection Rasmus Meyers, Bergen

8   MEUDON, 1890   Pastel on cardboard, 10½″ × 11¼″   Collection Kunstmuseum, Berne

image of the uncertainty, instability, and wavering movement of thought, in which the torment of anxious man originates and grows with an encroaching, confining power.

Munch relates the origin of this painting in a few lines written on the back of a lithograph of 1895 in which he repeated this theme.

«I was walking along the road with two friends. The sun set, and the sky turned blood red. I felt a touch of melancholy, and stopped and leaned against the railing, feeling extremely fatigued. Blood-red clouds and tongues of fire were floating above the city and the blue-black fjord. My friends kept on walking, but I stood still, trembling with anxiety. I felt as if I were hearing the immense, infinite cry of nature.»

This separation from his two friends, whose silhouettes we see in the background, accentuates the feeling of solitude into which the anxious man has plunged, as if to plumb the depths of his distress.

The ethical significance and the aesthetic implications of both figure and landscape are thus combined into a single «Expressionist» impulse. Later we shall see that on occasion Munch seems to have felt that landscape alone sufficed him as a tool for projecting into his painting the movements of an inner agitation. He was not the first painter to feel this way. His earliest precursor along this path is undoubtedly the late sixteenth-century painter El Greco, whose *View of Toledo* (Metropolitan Museum, New York) is a powerfully unreal, highly dramatized landscape in which a terrible storm seems to be threatening the city. El Greco did not hesitate to modify the position of the cathedral in relation to the castle, as if to highlight them better and so single out these two symbols of power for divine punishment.

Closer to our own time, the Expressionist landscape had its influential depictor in Van Gogh, whose mortal torments during the last two years of his life (1889–1890) sucked whirling skies and convulsed trees into a veritable pictorial delirium, as in his paintings of *The Olive Trees, Starry Night,* and *Cornfield with Crows.* But there were few Expressionist landscape painters during the first decades of the twentieth century; the principal ones are Erich Heckel, Karl Schmidt-Rottluff, August Macke, Otto Dix, Chaim Soutine, and a solitary Frenchman (who, however, was of Flemish origin), Vlaminck, and not one of them showed an exclusive preference for the landscape. As for the still life, which predominated in the works of those painters of reflection, the Cubists, it is completely absent from Expressionist painting. Not a single still life by Munch exists.

The precursors of Expressionism in the depiction of the human figure go back to a more distant past. A search for hints of it in an excess of expression given to a face leads us to the work of Hieronymus Bosch, to his *Ecce Homo* (Philadelphia Museum) and particularly to his *Carrying of the Cross* in the Ghent Museum. However, in fifteenth-century German painting the figures in this scene were traditionally depicted in caricatural form, and we find this done prior to Bosch, in the 1437 *Carrying of the Cross* in Hans Multscher's Wurzach altar (Berlin-Dahlem Museum). But that great lyrical, fundamentally Expressionist, movement that animates the *Crucifixion* in Matthias Grünewald's Isenheim altar (Colmar Museum) is missing from the Wurzach work. The Spanish school has its El Greco and its Goya, with their sometimes distorting emphasis placed on facial expression, but when all is said and done these are only isolated instances in the history of painting.

9

10   *Death and the Maiden, 1894   Drypoint, 11½″ × 8½″*

Thus, if we assign a place to Munch's work in relation to the Expressionist «movement,» which as we said is essentially a German movement, and when we recall that this movement did not begin until 1910, by which time Munch's Expressionist period was over, it is logical to regard the Norwegian painter — at least as regards those works that, like *The Scream,* were painted in the closing years of the nineteenth century — as a precursor of this form of expression, to which he contributed a major impetus.

A melancholy adolescence

The Munch family was a typical representative of the most responsible class of society in nineteenth-century Norway: its members were clergymen, army officers, teachers, doctors. It also included a painter (who was, however, a former officer of the Engineers' Corps), Jacob Munch, who, after taking lessons with David, became a traditional portraitist; and a dramatist, Andreas Munch. Christian Munch, Edvard's father, was a doctor in the Army Medical Corps.

At Christiania (the old Oslo), where his parents settled in 1864, Edvard's childhood was formed by his father's recitals of tales from the old sagas. Their mystery-laden adventures found their way into the book *Legends of the Gods and Heroes of the North,* by P. A. Munch, the professor-historian uncle whose works, read aloud during the long evenings of the Nordic winter, were a subject of family admiration.

Dr. Munch carefully supervised the education of his five children, Sophie, Edvard, Andreas, Laura, and Inger. But his financial difficulties, and the despondency caused by his wife's death from tuberculosis in 1868, when Edvard was five, left the household under the cloud of a distressing atmosphere. In 1877 Edvard's beloved fifteen-year-old sister Sophie died of the same disease. Edvard later left a moving souvenir of her in his painting *The Sick Child.* Thus there took shape, around and within him, that universe of sadness of which he was one day to say that «Illness, madness, and death are the dark angels who watched over my cradle and have accompanied me throughout my life.»

Madness? Undoubtedly it was only the edge of madness, if we are to see in the painter's words an allusion to the dark crisis of religious obsession that took possession of his father upon his mother's death. The father spent entire days, sometimes far into the night, in prayer in his room, something that terrified Edvard. As so often happens, his own obsessions were to enter his painting with images that plunge into his past and bring it back to life. That of his father appeared in 1902, in the woodcut *Old Man Praying.*

Other calamities overtook the Munch family, but the deaths of his mother and his sister Sophie had already had the effect of indicating to the future painter a special area in which his desire to express the impressions made upon him by life could be fulfilled. Thus he notes in his diary for November 8, 1880, «I am now determined to become a painter.»

His father wanted him to become an engineer, and with this in mind had registered him in 1879 at the Technical Institute. But Edvard spent little more than a year there. In 1881 he enrolled in the State School of Art and Handicraft, where he worked with Julius Middelthun and in 1882 studied painting under the direction of Christian Krohg.

Several works dating from this period, drawn with a somewhat academic diligence and painted with a rather austere palette, are still extant. They include several interior scenes, a view of Christiania, and two portraits that already reveal his power to express the complete character of a face with great sobriety of means. One of them, *Laura, Aged 14*, reappears in the foreground of a landscape of 1888 entitled *Evening Hour at Vrengen*, while his *Self-Portrait*, painted before he was 20, reveals somewhat stern good looks, which women found extremely attractive, although his timidity and shyness, and even at this early age a feeling of distrust that he never completely succeeded in overcoming, kept him at a distance from them.

These early works are not yet an augury of the path of his true personality. At most we find in them an undertone of melancholy in which his work was to find its inspiration. It sets the mood for portraits like that of his sister *Inger* (see page 13), which marks the end of his naturalistic period.

Paris and Berlin

Munch left Norway for the first time in 1885 to spend three weeks in Paris, a trip he owed to the generosity of his father's friend, the painter Frits Thaulow, who was one of the first to notice the young artist's talent, and who himself settled in Paris in 1896.

During his brief stay in Paris, Munch discovered not only the Louvre but also all the painters whose recent demonstrations had posed a serious challenge to official art. In 1885 the Impressionists were on the eve of their eighth and last exhibition. As in the case of Van Gogh, for whom they provided a decisive stimulus the following year, their works caused Munch to reconsider the problem of color. A change appeared in his painting from the date of his return to Christiania. The fact is that he now began to be in full command of himself.

From this period of 1885–1886 dates his first masterpiece, *The Sick Child*, an evocation of his feeling for his sister Sophie. He produced five versions of this subject; one is in the Nasjonalgalleriet in Oslo, another in the Tate Gallery in London, while the face alone, seen in profile against the pillow, was to reappear some ten years later in a drawing, an etching, and a lithograph. Munch's feelings had never before been expressed with such delicacy in the manner of applying his strokes of color to the canvas. There is nothing Expressionist about this painting; on the contrary, the muted poetic resonance of the vision of the young girl originates in a certain lack of precision in the drawing and a chaste abstention from any expression of feeling. The painter owes to Impressionism this freedom of treatment and subjective independence of color in relation to the form. «My work on *The Sick Child*» (see page 72), he wrote in connection with this picture, «cleared new paths for me, and opened a total breakthrough for my art. Most of my later works owe their origin to this painting.»

The same freedom is seen in two other paintings dating from 1885, *A Dance* (private collection, Oslo) and *Tête-à-Tête* (see page 16). In the latter painting a woman's face is visible through the veil of smoke rising from a pipe — a homey image whose delicacy is not always as wonderfully well expressed in the painter's work. It is strange to find that in this style, a direct outgrowth of Impressionism, Munch has made use of a palette of colors much darker than that of any Impressionist.

In the succeeding years, however, he turned away from this kind of dreamy vagueness that gives his paintings their profound charm. In 1889, the year of his first one-man exhibition of 110 works in Christiania, he painted a series of pictures in which he attempted to establish an intimate relationship between a figure and its surrounding

PORTRAIT OF INGER, THE ARTIST'S SISTER, 1892 Oil, 71⅝″ × 51″ Collection National Gallery, Oslo

KARL JOHAN STREET WITH MILITARY BAND, 1889   Oil, 42½″ × 59″
Collection Zürcher Kunstgesellschaft, Kunsthaus, Zurich

TÊTE-À-TÊTE, 1885   Oil, 27¼″ × 31½″   Collection Munch Museet, Oslo

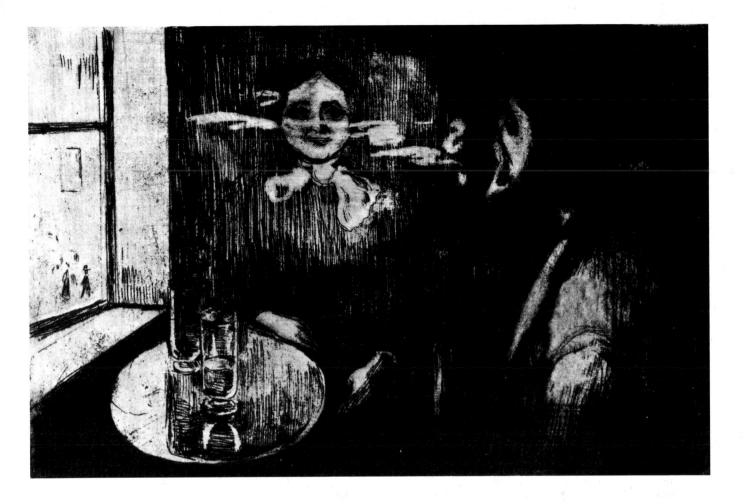

Tête à-tête, 1895   Drypoint and etching, 8″ × 12¼″

decor, whether a domestic interior or a landscape. The natural austerity of Munch's temperament is evident in the solemnity of the faces, but it has not yet become dramatic in nature. Silence, solitude, expectancy, and reverie are, as it were, caressed by the grace of a detail, a delicate lighting, a muted atmosphere.

In *Spring* (see page 5), one of the most representative paintings in this series, two women in dark clothes are seated in front of a window through which white voile curtains, puffed out by a slight breeze, are filtering the daylight. All the freshness of the northern spring is contained in this pale clarity that envelops the flowers placed on the window ledge. The two women, however, are still dressed in winter clothes. The distance that separates them from the window, the left side of the painting from the right, and shadow from light, contains the essential significance of the scene: the patient expectancy of two spectators before what is as yet only a promise of the arrival of summer.

In *An Evening Chat* (Statens Museum for Kunst, Copenhagen) the landscape seems to be guarding the couple's tryst, while in *Inger on the Shore* (Rasmus Meyer Collection, Bergen) it seems to give full measure to the young girl's solitude. These landscapes are not backgrounds installed behind portraits; rather, they are an extension into space of the spirit that constitutes the very nature of a meeting (a tryst) or a solitary reverie. Throughout his life Munch was concerned with imparting the echo of a cosmic meditation to his painting.

In this same year of 1889 Munch returned to France on a government scholarship. He remained there until 1892, living first in Paris, then in Saint-Cloud, and later visiting the Riviera. His desire to do serious work led him to choose as his teacher Léon Bonnat, the most serious — and most boring — of the official painters. Undoubtedly Munch was not impressed by his teacher's instruction, since he spent only four months in his studio. His discovery of various artistic movements that were very active in this year of the Universal Exhibition was of greater use to him. He was able to view the fourteen canvases by Manet appearing in the Centennial of French Art, the Gauguin works exhibited at the Café Volpini, paintings by Monet at the Georges Petit Gallery, the neo-Impressionist canvases of Seurat and his friends, and the debut of the Nabis, with Sérusier, Maurice Denis, Bonnard, Vuillard, Ranson, and others.

The very diverse tendencies represented by all these painters were to exert a more or less direct, but nevertheless temporary, influence on Munch. The most obvious influence is that of neo-Impressionism, which contributed its small, close strokes to several works he painted in 1891, although he did not rigorously apply the pointillist method. It is particularly evident in *Rue de Rivoli* (see page 23), *Rue Lafayette* (see page 22), and *Spring Day on Karl Johan Street* (Bergen Billedgalleri).

These, however, are merely superficial technical experiments. For Munch the matter of supreme importance, ranking even before the solution of the conflicting problems raised by the various styles of painting, was the subject of the painting: the *what* of painting will determine the *how* of painting. At Saint-Cloud, in 1889, he wrote in his diary with a kind of mystical fervor:

« We shall paint no more interiors with men reading or women knitting. They must be living beings who breathe, feel, suffer, and love. I shall paint a series of such paintings, and people will realize their religious nature and remove their hats before them, just as they do in church. »

18

The American Girl, 1894 Drypoint and etching, 5½″ × 4⅔″   19

The Kiss, 1898
Woodcut, 17″ × 19½″

The Kiss, 1895
Drypoint and aquatint, 12¹⁵/₁₆″ × 10³/₈″ ▷

20

22   RUE LAFAYETTE, 1891   Oil, 38⅓″ × 30½″   Collection National Gallery, Oslo

Rue de Rivoli, 1891   Oil, 32½″ × 26¼″   Collection Fogg Museum, Cambridge, Mass.   23

Munch added a tour of Italy to his trip, and then went to Germany. The Berlin of 1892, and the friendships he made there in artistic and literary circles, were of primary importance for him. He was less of a foreigner here than in France, for the reason that in Berlin Scandinavian artists were better known and appreciated. It is true that Ibsen's dramas had just been introduced into Paris. In 1890 *Ghosts* had been staged at the Théâtre Libre, to be followed in 1891 by *The Wild Duck*. In the same year *Hedda Gabler* was played at the Vaudeville, and in 1892 *The Lady from the Sea* at the Cercle des Escholiers. All these plays were published in translation, as were *Rosmersholm* and *An Enemy of the People,* staged by Lugné-Poe in 1893 at the Théâtre de l'Oeuvre, while Bjoernson's *The Bankrupt* and Strindberg's *Miss Julie* were to be played on the stage of the Théâtre Libre. But their audiences and their readers continued to form a very limited circle.

The Norwegian and Swedish intellectual achievements were much more firmly established in Berlin. However, the Germans were predisposed to welcome Scandinavia's dramatic literature much more than its painting. The first complete foreign edition of Strindberg's works was published in the German language. But in 1892 the group of Norwegians exhibiting with Munch at the Verein der Berliner Künstler (a predecessor of the Berlin Sezession) provoked a genuine scandal. The hostility of the critics and the public was so great that the exhibition had to close a week after it had opened.

It is still too early to speak of Expressionism. But the ideology that was to impregnate this movement several years later — a striking combination of symbolism and socialism, humanitarian ideas and mournful lyricism that is a hymn to Humanity and the City — was already taking shape in the Berlin literary circles in which Munch met the poets Richard Dehmel and Otto Julius Bierbaum, August Strindberg (whose portrait he painted in 1892), Julius Meier-Graefe (who contributed one of the four essays in Stanislaw Przybyszewski's *Das Werk von Edvard Munch,* the first book about the painter, published in Berlin in 1894), and Stanislaw Przybyszewski, a rather strange Polish author of works that are a blend of mysticism and satanism, a combination that inevitably exercised a powerful attraction on Munch's mind.

Przybyszewski's wife was a Norwegian woman named Dagny Juell — Duchna to her numerous close friends, among whom were Munch and Strindberg. Her laughter, it is said, drove men mad, and when combined with the inevitable drinking — she herself was an intrepid absinthe drinker — helped to create around the couple a frequently stormy atmosphere. The presence of all these men in love with the same woman, and the tension that existed among them, served Munch as an introduction to a new form of anxiety: jealousy. This seems to have placed yet another obstacle in the path of the flowering of his emotive faculties. In 1894–1895 it provided the title for a painting in which the principal figure, with its drawn face, has the features of the Polish writer. In *Jealousy* (see page 42), as in *The Scream,* the human being is confined within his solitude, which here is emphasized by the shadowy zone surrounding him. Munch did a less oppressive portrait of the writer in 1895, and the somber portrait of Duchna (*Dagny Juell Przybyszewska,* Oslo, Kommunes Kunstsamlinger), which he painted in 1893, appears to be an attempt (not a very successful one, it must be said) to capture the diabolical figure on canvas.

Duchna was to meet with a tragic end. She fled Berlin for Tiflis and (according to Meier-Graefe) a young Russian who, unable to endure her laughter, fired a revolver at

VAMPIRE, 1893   Oil, 37⅞″ × 45⅜″   Collection Munch Museet, Oslo

MELANCHOLY (THE YELLOW BOAT), c. 1891   Oil, 27$\frac{1}{12}$ × 40″   Collection National Gallery, Oslo

MOONLIGHT, 1893   Oil, 58½″ × 56¼″   Collection National Gallery, Oslo

Anxiety, 1894   Oil, 39″ × 30¼″   Collection Munch Museet, Oslo

THE SCREAM, 1893   Oil, 37⅞″ × 30⅝″   Collection National Gallery, Oslo

MADONNA, 1894   Oil, 37½″ × 29⅝″
Collection Hamburger Kunsthalle, Hamburg

THE DAY AFTER, 1894–95   Oil, 47⅞″ × 63⅜″
Collection National Gallery, Oslo

PUBERTY, 1894   Oil, 61⅝″ × 44⅝″   Collection National Gallery, Oslo

Puberty, 1903   Etching, 8¼" × 6⅔"   33

BATHING BOYS, c. 1895   Oil, 38⅓″ × 60¼″
Collection National Gallery, Oslo

34

SKETCH OF THE MODEL POSING, 1893   Pastel on cardboard, 30⅛″ × 20⅞″
Collection The Solomon R. Guggenheim Museum, New York

her point-blank before turning it upon himself. Duchna's end, like everything concerning the relationship between love and death, had profound and enduring repercussions on Munch's thought and work.

The theme of womanhood

It is obvious that this Berlin period, whose way of life Munch sought, upon his return to Norway, to find to some extent in the artistic circle known in Christiania as «Bohemia,» exerted a decisive influence on the painter's accession to his true personality. The paintings of 1893 are proof of this. First came *The Scream*, which we have already discussed and in which Munch completely departed from all his earlier styles of painting. Now liberated from any academic precision of draftsmanship, he was interested only in the movement of color as a means of emphasizing the dramatic character of the subject. Here he discovered a style that he was to repeat in *Madonna* (see page 30).

She is, to tell the truth, a strange madonna: a female nude whose mournful face is thrown back, and whose hair falls over her shoulders, while an orange circle forms a kind of halo around her head. Munch's ideological ambiguity concerning woman is openly expressed in this painting. Sometimes a virgin, at other times the incarnation of sin, in *Madonna* she appears as a synthesis of the painter's mystical and erotic urges. As early as 1893, in a drawing that he titled *Madonna*, a woman's face had appeared in profile in the center of a circular area reminiscent of a nimbus. Despite the sensuality of the line, the nudity was chaste. In one of five later versions of this subject, however, drawn on stone in 1895 and metamorphosed into a color lithograph in 1902, he makes the meaning of the picture crudely clear. This time the same female torso with its shining flesh is framed by tears of sperm, while a fetus is placed in one corner of the composition. Its subtitle is *Ideal Representation of the Moment of Conception*.

It is significant that in this same year of 1894 Munch painted two pictures in which the theme of womanhood is treated in two different aspects that for him are like the twin poles of a physiological and spiritual evolution. The first one is entitled *Puberty* (see page 32), and shows a little girl seated naked on her bed, an anxious question written across her face. In the second, *Vampire* (see page 25), a man bends over to bury his face in the bosom of the woman holding him in her arms, while she too bends forward to bite him in the nape of the neck. This image of woman as desired and feared, seductive and destructive, is at the heart of the anxieties that made Munch for a long time the victim of his personal hell. In this he bears a strong resemblance to Strindberg, whose misogyny, encouraged by his marital disappointments and complicated, as in Munch's case, by constant ambivalence, caused him to depict woman in his writings as Madonna and as Vampire.

In an 1894 engraving, *Harpy*, Munch repeated this theme in another form in which the harpy, half woman and half bird, stands over the cadaver of a man. He later composed a lithograph, *Poison Flower*, as an illustration for the fable *Alpha and Omega*, in which the flower at the top of its stalk is a trefoil female head. In many of his drawings and engravings, too, we find a woman accompanied by a skeleton. In a watercolor of 1896–1897 entitled *In the Cemetery*, and somewhat reminiscent of the features of the *Madonna* and her halo, a woman walks among the graves, while a tiny skeleton, similarly haloed and bearing two arrows, the symbols of love, appears near her.

Lovers in the Waves, 1896   Lithograph, 13⁵/₁₂″ × 18″

Here we should perhaps establish a distinction between two aspects of Munch's mental life that at a certain point are superimposed in his artistic creation. On the one hand, woman is depicted as the instrument of man's destruction, and as having deadly power over him. On the other hand, the apparently very strong duality of his life instinct and his death instinct caused him to conceive a kind of successful union between Eros and Thanatos, expressed in an etching of 1894, *Maiden and Death* (see page 10), in which we see a beautiful young female nude and a skeleton, in standing position, tenderly embracing.

Munch personally appears in this iconography of woman whom he regards as a being to be feared. In 1893, in his *Self-Portrait under Female Mask*, he depicts himself with a face set in an expression of sadness, fear, and disgust. The woman's face above him is a terrifying sight, with its oversized mouth and immense, coallike eyes. As always, however, this woman is simultaneously deadly and desired. That same year, in his picture

DEATH IN THE SICK CHAMBER, 1893–94   Oil, 62½″ × 70″
Collection National Gallery, Oslo

JEALOUSY, 1894–95   Oil, 27⅞″ × 41⅞″
Collection Rasmus Meyers, Bergen

ASHES, 1894   Oil, 50¼″ × 58¾″
Collection National Gallery, Oslo

Rose and Amélie, 1894   Oil, 32$\frac{1}{2}$″ × 45$\frac{5}{12}$″   Collection Munch Museet, Oslo

entitled *Hands,* he painted a female nude surrounded by hands stretching out toward her. Two years later he created a lithograph version, subtitled *Lust toward Woman.* These hands in truth resemble flames, but are they devouring or purifying? They reappear around 1895 in his self-portrait *In Hell,* an irresistible plunge by Munch into his own depths and torments, which left him with a fondness for exploring and translating into paint the torments and troubles of other people and of humanity as a whole. In this he resembles Ibsen, who has one of the characters in *The Wild Duck* say, « It is good to plunge occasionally into the dark side of life. »

The engraver and lithographer

Munch's first graphic works date from 1894. He began with dry point, but quickly became interested in technical experiments and, like Goya, combined etching and aquatint on the same plate. Using this method, and treating the surface of the copper with resin, he was able to obtain a washlike appearance in which the drawing is partially accentuated by the bite of the acid. Sometimes, as in the first version of *The Sick Child,* he combines aquatint and dry point, while in *The Kiss* (in which a nude man and a woman, standing, embrace in front of a window) all three methods are combined (see pages 20 and 21).

He used lithography and the woodcut to translate the principal subjects of his painting into prints. Thus each theme is repeated in several versions that involve variations and sometimes a change of title. Munch has been charged with carelessness in limiting his printings. Approximately seventeen thousand printings have been made of the 800-odd plates he bequeathed to the city of Oslo. For Munch, however, the success of whose painting always ended at the frontiers of his native land, the print was a more certain means of publicizing his work.

He returned to France (chiefly Paris, but he also stopped in Nice) in 1895 and 1896, and exhibited at the Salon des Indépendants, the Salon de l'Art Nouveau, and Bing's Gallery. The new trends being welcomed by Bing to his gallery were to be reflected in Munch's painting and lithographs, particularly in *Jealousy* (1896), one of the themes he depicted in a number of versions, and the subject of an article published by his friend Strindberg in *La Revue Blanche.* Several Parisian publishers now became aware of Munch's work. The lithograph *Anxiety,* printed in black and red by Clot, was published by Vollard under the title (subsequently abandoned) of *Evening* in his first *Album des Peintres Graveurs,* while the Cent Bibliophiles commissioned him to illustrate an edition of *Flowers of Evil.*

He became friendly with Stéphane Mallarmé, and did two portraits of him, one engraved in soft varnish, the other a lithograph (see page 49). In a letter of June 15, 1896, Mallarmé thanks him for the « discerning portrait in which I intimately feel my own presence. » In the same year a Munch lithograph illustrated the program for Ibsen's *Peer Gynt* (see page 75), played at the Théâtre de l'Oeuvre. A portrait of August Strindberg done by the same method also dates from 1896 (see page 48).

Munch experimented with interesting innovations in the woodcut technique, to which he devoted a great deal of time during his stay in Paris. Some of his prints combine wood block, stone, and zinc plate, that is, a combination of xylography and lithography. He also engraved zinc in sufficient depth to produce relief prints. Using two or three wooden blocks for color printings, he obtained interesting effects through the contrast

Melancholy, 1899   Lithograph, 20" × 22⅞"

of crude chisel work and extremely refined coloring. An example of this is *Moonlight* (1896), in which he repeated the subject of an 1893 painting: a female figure standing in front of a wooden house. (In the engraving the composition is reversed, as is generally the case in works by Munch, who used his designs without concern for the reversal caused by the transferral from the plate to the paper.) The painter's interest in these graphic works increased with the passing years, and they continued to form a major and by no means less original part of his work.

A new style

The years between 1892 and 1898 constitute the period of the affirmation of Munch's most personal character, the period in which he created his major works. His development, however, did not follow an unbroken line. Perhaps he was somewhat uncertain about his aesthetic research; perhaps he wanted to pursue various technical experiments simultaneously. In any event, within a single year we find him painting works in different styles and with a variety of treatments. This makes our task more difficult when we attempt to grasp the essence underlying the instability of Munch's activity.

Thus it is surprising that a canvas like *Spring Evening on Karl Johan Street, Oslo* (see page 15), in which a new, extremely original, and extremely Expressionist style appears, was painted in 1892, that is, one year before *Puberty* and prior to the portrait *Dagny Juell Przybyszewska*, the style of which is so much closer to the less coloristic canvases of the preceding years. We would be tempted to believe in an error of dating but for the reappearance, in 1894–1895, of pictures like *The Day After* (see page 31), the style of which is similar to that of *Puberty*.

One apparent interpretation of this procedure of «three steps forward, two steps back» is that Munch experienced significant difficulty in tearing himself away from his past, to which he returns in his style of painting and his repetition of subjects he had painted in his youth. The most typical example in this connection is his *Two Women on the Shore* (1935; Munch Museet, Oslo), a repetition — in greatly impoverished style — of a theme of 1898.

We must therefore discern an aesthetic movement in his development that, by its pictorial quality and the number of works it produced, dominates all his other works painted, so to speak, against the current. This movement begins in 1892 with *Spring Evening on Karl Johan Street*, continues in 1893 with *The Scream* and *Death in the Sick Chamber* (see page 41), and continues with a certain number of canvases painted between these dates and 1908, which we shall now examine. (What happened after 1908 is another matter, and will be discussed later.)

Munch's new style, which appeared in 1892, imparts a very precise meaning to the word *Expressionism* and what it meant for him: the statement of an emotion, the capturing of a paroxysmal moment in which we are *given a glimpse* of an inner upheaval the secret of which is not revealed by its image. For Munch conceals from us the reason for this emotion. We never learn what has motivated the action of *The Scream*. In *Death in the Sick Chamber* the patient remains invisible in his distant bed surrounded by grieving members of his family. And we are given no information about the reasons for the anxiety on the faces, seen in frontal view, of the strollers in *Spring Evening on Karl Johan Street*. Here the anxiety is not «cried out»; it remains silent, hence all the more disturbing. In the distance, the lighted windows of a house seem to complement the unusual lighting of the wan faces.

This kind of modesty in the rejection of any explanation — perhaps out of the artist's fear of revealing the reasons for his own anxiety — added to the mystery of the composition, gives Munch's works a resonance that is missing from the works of the other Expressionists.

The figures in *Spring Evening on Karl Johan Street* reappear in 1894 in the painting entitled *Anxiety,* and in an 1896 lithograph, *Feeling of Anxiety,* which we prefer to the

48

A closer examination of [...]
them if we consider the consist
symbols of a persistent obsessio
its very unusual shape, always
Voice (Museum of Fine Arts, B
trees and the young woman stan
of the same subject and in two
turned up in *The Dance of Lif*
«acknowledged» ten years late
Chemistry, one of the decorativ
motif appears yet again in 190(
Shore, in 1907 in *The Moon* an
representing three women on a
side of the composition. To con
reflection is included in several

The landscape painter

The aesthetic characteris
personal echo, stripped of any
the painters who were propag
Sérusier, Ranson, Vallotton, and
work, but his forms have becor
the colors arranged in simplified
He painted his best lar
page 86), *Winter Night* (see bac
(Munch Museet, Oslo) — aroun
interesting personality as a colo
blue, places his landscapes bey
with such great power of evoca
special time of day — one of t
instance, when the unusual clar
the nocturnal shadows — that a
contemplation of nature, is esta
Moreover, it is strange t
from the groups revolving in
landscapes, which are stamped
himself have daydreamed for n
Norway (as I have done durin
to which a fir tree can suddenl
shape, ready to spring to life ir
landscapes so disturbing: a sile
plant life.
Among the themes he tr
provided the occasion for a ser
the same style (that of *The Dan*

August Strindberg,
1896
Lithograph, 20″ × 14½″
◁

Stéphane Mallarmé
1896
Lithograph, 16⅔″ × 12″

Henrik Ibsen in the

canvas because of its mo~
transposed into the fjord (

These constant trans
components of a work, cha
a subject was not exhausted
are not the principal subjec
that tends to establish a fu
those to which all human b
dimensions of an allegorica

Thus *Laura* (1899), t~
and morose couples dancin
pages 58 and 59).

with a change of figures or a difference in their positions. The three girls are first seen from behind, leaning on the railing and looking into the water, in which the green mass of a large tree is reflected (see page 69). One is blond, another a brunette, and the third a redhead, as if Munch wished to synthesize all the natures of woman. (Later we shall see the importance Munch attached to women's hair.) In a 1900 version (Kunsthalle, Hamburg), one of the girls has turned around. *Women on the Jetty* (Thielska Galleriet, Stockholm) shows us a group of women in the middle of the bridge. All these canvases were painted in Aasgaardstrand, a coastal village on the Oslo fjord, which Munch visited for the first time in 1889, and to which he often returned to work. The bridge theme was to return more than once, even after 1930, in a total of about a dozen painted and engraved works on the subject.

This style, however, with its simplified forms and rather pale colors, apparently did not suit Munch for all the subjects he painted. He had tried to apply it to a not very successful canvas, *The Dead Mother* (between 1896 and 1899). He repeated the subject around 1900 (Kunsthalle, Bremen), under the same title but in a more realistic style, and here he achieved a great dramatic intensity by depicting the terrified little girl with her back to the bed on which her mother lies and holding her hands to her ears (in a gesture similar to that of the person in *The Scream* as if death is for her a funereal music that she cannot bear to hear).

Similarly, when he paints a portrait (and throughout his life he was an excellent portrait painter), Munch forgets this symbolizing tendency, in which each form contributes its share of movement to the general arabesque of the painting, in order to concentrate all his attention on the expression of a face. His aesthetic system had nevertheless evolved since the austere portraits of his sisters Laura and Inger, painted between 1881 and 1884.

Munch's favorite model, the one to which he always returned, was himself, and he left innumerable self-portraits. He seems to question this face more intensely in each one, as if hoping to discover in it something new about his own tormented nature.

He had begun painting his own portrait in 1880, during his first year of art studies. The second self-portrait dates from 1881–1882, when Munch was not yet twenty. In it he is handsome Edvard, with features full of a romantic melancholy to which the severe style of the picture is well suited. By 1886 the treatment had become much more free, almost that of a sketch, except for the essential features of the face — the eyes, nose, and mouth — which he worked out more thoroughly. In 1895 a different man appears in the very beautiful *Self-Portrait with Cigarette* (see page 57). Maturity has changed the features; the lips are shadowed by a small moustache, and Munch's gaze has acquired a rather peculiar look that is emphasized by the somewhat eerie lighting of the face. This portrait can be regarded as a prefiguration of the self-portrait *In Hell* (Oslo, Kommunes Kunstsamlinger), which we have already discussed.

At this time Munch was preoccupied with the tragic side of life. For him, the true meaning of life was understood only in its orientation toward death. A lithograph *Self-Portrait* of 1895 has a black background and the skeleton of an arm at the bottom of the picture. Perhaps he had seen the 1889 engraving by James Ensor in which the Belgian painter had depicted himself in the form of a skeleton. In any event, the strange thing is that Munch conceived this skeleton depiction of his own hand seven years prior to the day on which he actually lost a finger joint from his left hand during a violent argument to which we shall refer later. (This almost premonitory event can be compared with the case of Victor Brauner, who in 1938 lost his left eye, under similar circumstances, six years

SIN (NUDE WITH
RED HAIR), 1901
Colored lithograph
$20\frac{5}{8}'' \times 16\frac{5}{8}''$

53

54   *Madonna (The Brooch), 1903   Lithograph, 23⅝″ × 18⅛″*

Salomé (Eva Mudocci and Munch), 1903   Lithograph, 16⅞″ × 12¾″   55

56   Ragnar Bäckström, 1894   Pastel, 36¼″ × 29⅛″   Private collection, Oslo

SELF-PORTRAIT WITH CIGARETTE, 1895   Oil, 46″ × 35⅝″   Collection Munch Museet, Oslo

DANCE OF LIFE
1899–1900
Oil, 52¼″ × 79⅜″
Collection
National Gallery
Oslo

58

RED VIRGINIA CREEPER, c. 1900   Oil, 54″ × 50⅜″   Collection Munch Museet, Oslo

after painting a *Self-Portrait with Missing Eye* and a complete series of pictures composed around the theme of ocular mutilation.)

Philosophy, literature, and Symbolist poetry all play an important role in Munch's painting. He saw himself as the poet of the great poem of life, and as such he depicts himself in *Self-Portrait with Lyre,* a very beautiful drawing of 1897–1898. For several years, especially after 1893, he had been dreaming of a large fresco on a theme dear to his heart, that of Love and Death, for which he made numerous sketches. In 1902 a composition took shape that was to become *The Frieze of Life,* and on which he was to spend many years working. The composition, divided into four parts — *Birth of Love, Bloom and Decay of Love, Fear of Life,* and *Death* — summarizes in one vast synthesis all the ideas and torments that dominated his entire life. As we have seen, many of his pictures are tentative approaches to or echoes of this theme. Moreover, he established a link binding together all his pictures, saying that in order to fully understand his work it was helpful to look at several pictures in juxtaposition, since their significance was better revealed by simultaneous study of the group.

However, the desire to achieve a major ideological work often led Munch to concentrate his attention on the symbolic content of this work, to the detriment of its pictorial expression. We prefer the less ambitious canvases, born of his passionate observation of the simple scenes of intimate life, and which, unbeknownst to him, are in their own way the isolated fragments of a more interesting «frieze of life.»

This is the case with a canvas of 1890, in its 1894–1895 version (the original was destroyed by fire): *The Day After* (see page 31). In the image of this woman stretched out on her bed, her unbound hair falling toward the floor, with glasses and bottles on a table in the foreground, there is none of the anecdotal realism that such a subject might imply. The impression of an unbalanced life and thinking deranged by drunkenness emanates with spellbinding power from the simple linear schema on which the painting is built: a surging movement of curves and oblique lines in which the eye searches in vain for a straight line on which to rest.

The portraitist

Closer to the style of his landscapes, and, like them, richer in color, is the new portrait of his sister Laura (Nasjonalgalleriet, Oslo) that Munch painted around 1900 under the title (repeated on several occasions) of *Melancholia.* The girl is seated idly in front of a table on which stands a pot of flowers. Her back is toward the windows of the room, and her gaze is fixed on a dream that is fascinating her, and which, translated through the medium of her face, fascinates us in turn, just as we are overwhelmed by the very prostration Laura seems to be distractedly suffering because of her solitude.

In the large full-length portraits painted in the early years of this century, Munch sometimes reflects of Manet, for whom he had acquired a profound admiration in Paris. Solidly built up and broadly painted, they express the model's character with great perspicacity. «I am able to see the person behind the mask,» Munch stated. In 1901 he painted the portraits *Hermann Schlittgen* and *Monsieur Archimard* also known, respectively, as *The German* and *The Frenchman* (see page 81). In 1903 he did two female portraits — *Aase Noerregaard* and *The Actress Ingse Vibe Müller.* These were followed in 1904 by *Max Linde* and *Count Kessler,* the latter a bust view in front of the count's library.

61

Lübeck, 1902   Etching, 20³/₅″ × 26⁷/₈″

Two years later Munch painted two other portraits of this German Maecenas who, in 1908, took Maillol to Greece, a trip from which the sculptor derived tremendous educational benefits.

The year of 1904 is also the year of a new *Self-Portrait* in which the painter appears dressed in an elegant frock coat and holding his brushes in his hand. In 1905 he made an etching of Gustav Schiefler, the man who in 1923 was to publish in Dresden a major book on Munch's graphic work. *Nietzsche* and *Elisabeth Förster-Nietzsche* were the chief portraits of 1906, *Ernest Thiel* and *Walter Rathenau* those of 1907. With the exception of Mr. Archimard, the painter's patrons were almost all German or Norwegian.

Nearly all these portraits are treated in the same vigorous style that at the time must have seemed reasonably «modernistic.» In 1907 he began a series of nudes in a more daring style, in which he seems to return, in a very personal manner, to an Impressionist vision. In *Consolation* (in which a man holds a weeping woman in his arms), *Amor and Psyche*, and the strange *Marat's Death* (in which a nude woman stands in front of a death bed), the entire canvas is painted with long, vertical, very visible strokes and juxtaposed colors that give the sensation of a vibration of light, as is sometimes seen (but with less systematic application) in some of Toulouse-Lautrec's oil paintings on cardboard, particularly in his *Woman with Black Boa* and *Woman with Gloves*. In general, however, Munch's studies of nudes, which became quite numerous at this period, cannot be ranked among his best works.

He is more interesting when he permits his ideas on the nature of woman to appear through his engravings and lithographs. Munch, who lived in an age in which women still kept their long hair, always saw in it both an attribute of their beauty and a dangerous instrument of seduction in which men are trapped as in a net. The drawing entitled *The Kiss of Death,* in which a death's head embraces a woman whose long hair is entwined around its skeletal neck, is an extremely violent expression of his pessimistic vision. In less macabre fashion, *The Vampire* (1894) and *Sin* (1901) are symbolized by

Westminster Abbey, 1912   Lithograph, 10⅛″ × 16⅔″

women with long red hair falling over their shoulders. This is consistent with the fact that Munch was always strongly attracted to red-haired women. We shall later examine a particular case in which this attraction was reversed, in his behavior, into flight.

In a series of lithographs done in 1896, *Attraction I* (see page 38), *Attraction II*, *Liberation I* (see page 39), and *Liberation II*, woman's hair seems to embody in concrete form the emotional bond that is created or broken between man and woman. In *Attraction* they are facing each other, and the woman's long hair envelops the man's shoulders. *Liberation* brings a certain distance between the two beings; they turn their backs on each

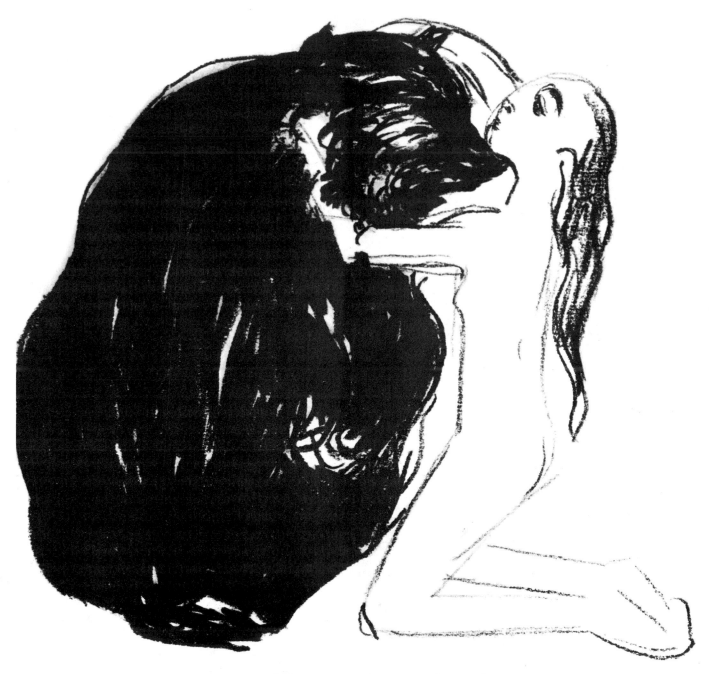

Omega and the Bear, Lithograph, 8¹⁄₈″ × 8¹⁄₃″

other, but the now unusually long hair crosses this space horizontally and breaks loose from the man's shoulders. These images can be compared with a color woodcut of the same year entitled *Man's Head Entangled in a Woman's Hair* and a lithograph, also of 1896, entitled *Lovers in the Waves* (see page 40), in which the man's head rests on the shoulder of a woman whose hair, floating over the waves, follows their undulating movement.

In moments of more serene sensuality, the long, flowing locks merely participate in the idealization of the beloved woman. When in 1903 Munch did the portrait of the English violinist Eva Mudocci, entitled *Madonna—the Brooch* (see page 54) and one of his most beautiful lithographs, he drew her luminous face, framed in the black flood of her hair, with visible love. She appears again in *The Violin Concert,* drawn with the same admiring tenderness. Suddenly, however, she is identified with her criminal sisters in a lithograph in which the head of Munch himself rests on the shoulder of the violinist, whose hair falls over the painter's forehead. The title of the print, *Salome,* makes its meaning abundantly clear (see page 55).

The crisis of 1908

Munch's anguished nature, his inner conflicts, emotional difficulties, and obsessions, so often reflected in his art, to say nothing of his tendency to alcoholism, undoubtedly predisposed him toward the crisis that in the fall of 1908 brought him to Professor Jacobson's neurological clinic in Copenhagen for a sojourn of seven or eight months. Munch's psychological problems seem not to have been the subject of very enlightened study by his biographers. They are satisfied to speak in vague terms of a «nervous crisis» or «depression,» without supplying any information about its true nature and without examining any medical records.

Since we were unsuccessful in our efforts to obtain precise documentation on this question from the Munch Archives, we must limit ourselves to a tentative explanation, which is not sufficient to precisely define the pathological characteristics of his case, but which will enable us to understand some of the links established between his behavior and certain peculiarities of his aesthetic system.

We have seen that in the events of his life, as well as in his most consistent ideological preoccupations, death played a major role as a source of anxiety and as a stimulus to his creative activity. Among the events that operated within this dual perspective, the tragic death of Dagny Juell Przybyszewska had left an indelible mark on him. Another event to which we must refer is an episode in his life that occurred in the fall of 1902.

Munch was then living in Aasgaardstrand. For more than four years he had been trying to escape from a relationship with a young Norwegian woman, about whom we know only that she had red hair, was the daughter of a rich businessman in Christiania, and, being madly in love with the painter, was determined to marry him. But he stubbornly refused, for the reason, he said, that her position as a wealthy woman was humiliating for him with his still very uncertain resources. To achieve her purpose, she concocted a plot with the help of some of Munch's friends. One day his friends came to tell him that she was dead. They took the painter by boat to the other bank of the fjord, and to a house in Droebak. The young woman's seemingly lifeless body, with her long red

WOMEN ON THE BEACH, 1898 Woodcut

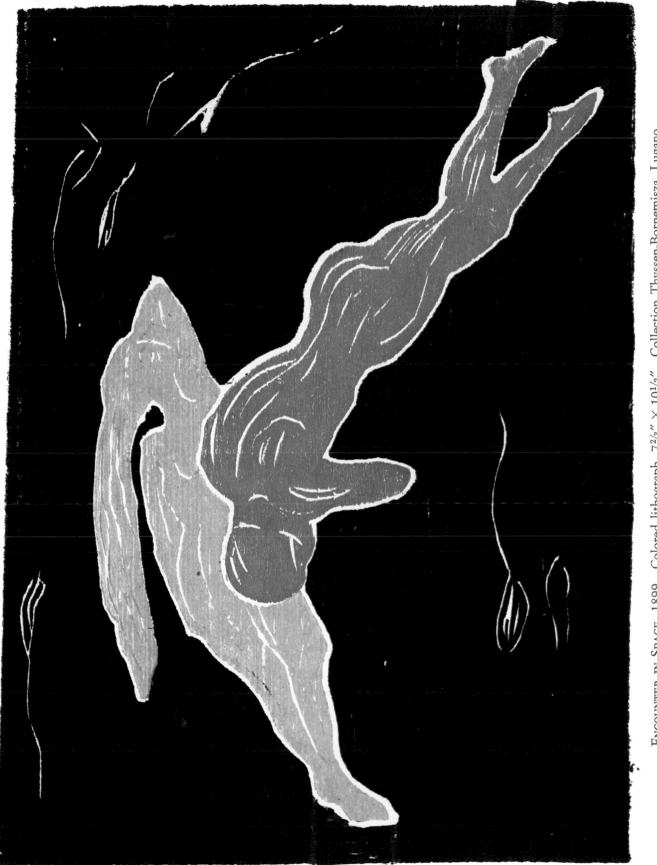

ENCOUNTER IN SPACE, 1899   Colored lithograph, 7²⁄₃″ × 10¹⁄₂″   Collection Thyssen-Bornemisza, Lugano

hair falling over her shoulders, was lying on a bed in the room in which the macabre setting had been prepared. Munch gazed with great emotion at the woman he had loved. But when she suddenly sat up, convinced that in his joy at seeing her «resurrected» he would no longer refuse to marry her, he took it amiss, furious at the trick they had played on him.

Upon his return to Aasgaardstrand a violent argument broke out between him and his friends, during which a shot was fired, wounding Munch in the left hand and leading to the loss of a finger joint when surgery was performed at the Christiania hospital. The effects of this drama remained with Munch for some years. It was as if all his customary reasons for seeing in woman the incarnation of the spirit of evil had now been justified and proven. Throughout his life he remained single.

Apart from the special mental climate this reveals, a consideration of Munch's aggressive nature sheds light on the consequences of the Droebak affair. The quarrel at Aasgaardstrand was not an isolated incident. In 1904 he created a scandal in Copenhagen by arguing in public with the writer Andreas Haukland. In 1905 he had a nasty quarrel with the painter Ludvig Karsten, whose portrait he had painted that same year. If we accept the idea that aggressiveness is an outward manifestation of the death instinct, and that an obsession with persecution is a projection onto others of one's own aggressiveness, it is understandable that Munch ultimately sank into a permanent state of fear and distrust of those around him, in which his friends became his «enemies,» eager to persecute him.

A few echoes of his sojourn at Professor Jacobson's clinic appear in drawings, prints, and a portrait of Jacobson done in 1909. In *The Madwoman,* a lithograph of 1908–1909, a standing woman seems to be talking with her shadow, which rises before her. Munch also did the portrait of the professor's assistant, Miss Schacke, in a very pretty dry-point profile entitled *The Nurse,* and illustrated the tale *Alpha and Omega* in a series of amusing drawings, a rather surprising work to come from the hand of an artist so little inclined toward humor. Lastly, he did his own portrait, in lithograph and paint, and that of the Danish author Helge Rode.

Thus his stay at the clinic did not interrupt his artistic activity for any length of time. Shortly after his cure he undertook a long series of major works, and his disturbances apparently never returned.

Nevertheless, we have some reason to believe that his crisis of 1908 was a serious one, and that it marks a total break in the development of his work.

We know very little about his medical treatment in Copenhagen. A caricature of him made at the clinic does not supply much information. Munch has depicted himself seated near a table on which stand two electrical apparatuses. Near him a nurse — undoubtedly Miss Schacke — holds a wire leading from one of these devices, and she is handing it to Professor Jacobson, who applies the end to the painter's head. At the top of the page are three lines in Munch's handwriting: «Professor Jacobson is electrifying the famous painter Munch, and is bringing a positive masculine force and a negative feminine force to his fragile brain.» The fanciful explanation given here by Munch — and the reference to his personal ideas on the positive-negative antagonism of the sexes — nevertheless leads us to believe that he was subjected to the application of one of those methods that, long before the practice of electroshock (which was then unknown), attempted to treat by electricity certain diseases that today would be treated with psychiatric and psychoanalytic techniques.

GIRLS ON A JETTY, 1901   Oil, 56⅝″ × 52¼″   Collection National Gallery, Oslo

GIRLS ON THE BEACH, 1903–04   Oil, 37½″ × 61⅝″
Collection Hamburger Kunsthalle, Hamburg

70

THE SICK CHILD, 1906–07   Oil, 46¾″ × 47⅝″   Collection Tate Gallery, London

PROPS FOR A SCENE OF IBSEN'S "GHOSTS,"
Collection Munch Museet, Oslo

74

Munch also alludes to this in a letter written from the clinic to his friend Jaffe Nilsson.

« I was on the verge of cracking up. You remember at Grand six years ago — you had noticed how far gone I was, and since then I have been doing nothing but existing in a state of tension and anxiety, which just had to burst out. And the outbreak was violent. After a trip to Sweden and after four days with Sigurd Mathiesen in the paradise of alcohol I had a genuine nervous depression and probably a slight attack — when you're constantly going over and over the same thing in your mind the brain is damaged. They're giving me electrical treatments and massages, and I'm making a good recovery in the peace and quiet, cared for by lovable nuns and a friendly doctor. »

If we look at Munch's entire output during his long development (in 1909 he had 35 years of life ahead of him), we are obliged to say that everything in his painting that bears the mark of his genius — that plunge into the dark recesses of the human being, which he expresses with a gripping power, those portraits in which the model's thought seems to be laid bare by his scrutinizing eye, those landscapes in which the outbreak and sadness of winter echo each other like the successively charming and poignant motifs of a symphony — was done before 1908.

To be sure, in later years we still encounter an interesting painting or a pretty watercolor from time to time, but nothing truly remarkable was to be added in the work he constantly produced, nothing new in the basic personality his work revealed. He occasionally repeated his early themes, as if to renew his links with his past, but he was never again to recover that quality that had made them profoundly original.

Did he himself have the feeling that something had changed in his powers of expression? Or was he thinking only of his behavior in life when he wrote that he viewed his stay at the clinic « as the end of one period of my life »? But he had also written, with great lucidity, « These weaknesses that I shall retain are part of me. I should not want to reject my illness, because my art owes a great deal to it. »

Aesthetic disorder

The first two paintings by Munch to reveal in extremely striking fashion a break with his pictorial past are the *Portrait of Professor Jacobson* and the *Self-Portrait in a Blue Suit,* both painted in 1909. In order to understand what differentiates them completely from the paintings that had brought the artist's personality to fruition prior to 1908, it must be observed that in the earlier paintings — both the most typically Expressionist ones and those in which he tended toward an older, more classical style — Munch's work always had the appearance of a painting executed in an atmosphere of reflection. His attention to the general movement of the composition, the harmony of the colors, and the technique of the stroke testified to an aesthetic system under complete mastery. Munch's disturbed, anxious, pessimistic nature was constantly in evidence, but it was not violent. On the contrary: in the works of his most coloristic period (*The Virginia Creepers* see page 60), the 1900 portrait *Laura,* the landscapes of 1900–1902, sometimes bordering on the Art Nouveau style) a certain softness dominated form.

Now, however, the painting suddenly gushed forth onto the canvas in a ruthless and disorderly manner. The rapid, broad brush strokes in which the color is crushed on

NIETZSCHE, 1905–06   Oil, 83⅓″ × 54⅙″   Collection Munch Museet, Oslo

NUDE RECLINING, 1912–13   Oil, 33⅜″ × 41⅝″   ANNA, 1920   Oil, 62½″ × 44″ ▷
Collection Hamburger Kunsthalle, Hamburg   Collection Marlborough Fine Art Ltd., London

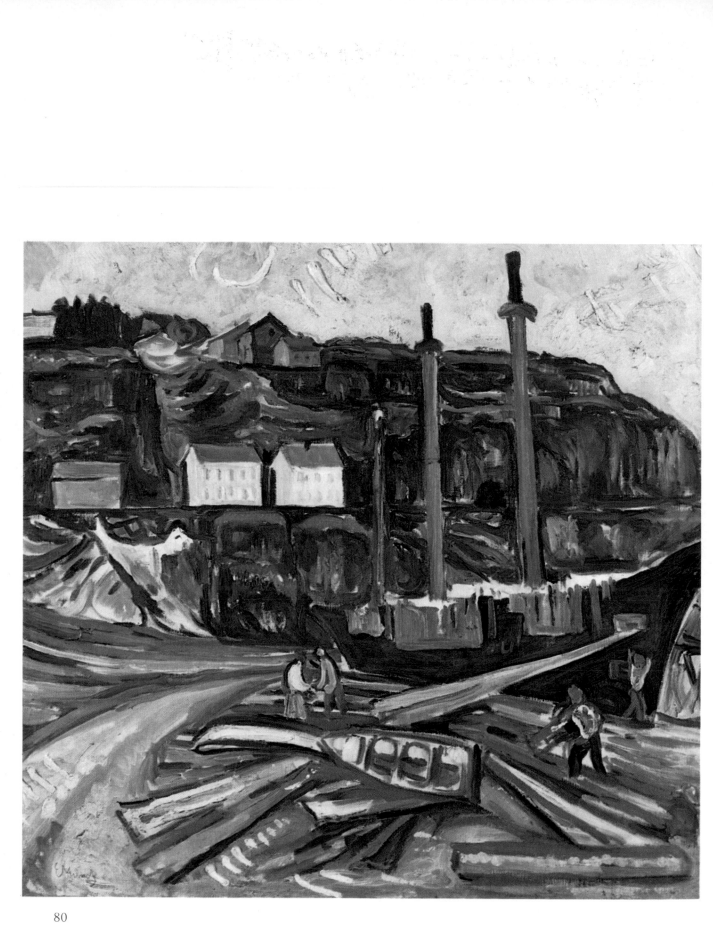

80

THE FRENCHMAN,
MONSIEUR ARCHIMARD, 1901
Oil, 76⅝″ × 29⅛″
Collection National Gallery
Oslo
▷

◁

WHARF, THE SHIP IS
DISMANTLED, 1911
Oil, 45⅝″ × 41¼″
Collection Zürcher Kunstgesellschaft,
Kunsthaus, Zurich

81

Galloping Horse, 1915   Etching, $15^5/_6'' \times 13^5/_8''$

in abrupt impastos produced the fulgurating vision of the *Portrait of Professor Jacobson* (Munch Museet, Oslo). This energy, to which we were not accustomed on the part of this painter, makes an irritating impression on us by the strange disharmony of the coloring, in which reds, yellows, oranges, greens, and blacks are most unsuccessfully juxtaposed. We are far from the daring but not clashing chromatism of *The Scream,* and still farther from the refinement of *The Sick Child.*

The same is true of the *Self-Portrait in a Blue Suit* (Rasmus Meyer Collection, Bergen), in which the painter's face is as if mangled by splashes of color. It is as if the violence of which we find numerous examples in Munch's life, and of which he had been cured by his sojourn at the clinic, had been suddenly carried over into his painting. But if such a process was beneficial for his mental condition, it was to the detriment of his art.

He himself had begun the tranquil life for which the clinic had been an apprenticeship. He emphasized its conditions with a certain humor and, perhaps, a touch of sadness: «Cigars without nicotine — drinks without alcohol — women without sex.» In a letter to his aunt he showed a resolve to choose the path of wisdom:

I also see very clearly that I must make a systematic effort to overcome my nervous weakness, which is a consequence of the years of persecution by that evil woman. I have finally understood that all my violent scenes were simply the morbid expression of those sufferings that lasted for so many years. I wish to find a corner of absolute tranquillity so that I can paint in peace.

He found, or thought he found, this corner of «absolute tranquillity» first at Skrubben, near Krageroe, where he stayed during the winter of 1910 and the spring of 1911, and then at Hvitsten, where he worked for a time. Ultimately he settled at Ekely, in the suburbs of Oslo, where in 1916 he purchased a piece of land, and where he was to die.

Yet the works he painted from this time on were extraordinarily agitated in style. *Children in the Street* (1910; Munch Museet, Oslo) combines all the characteristics of this agitation: painting without draftsmanship and without structure, and bright color consisting in large part of pure paint hurled onto the canvas in broad, thick, isolated stains. The same chaotic dispersion appears in *The Murderer* (1911; Munch Museet, Oslo), in which the trails of light and dark paint seem to have been applied haphazardly, and the central figure with its green face and red hands stands out against a landscape background that has been roughly sketched in.

The best of these unrestrained paintings is the *Galloping Horse* of 1912 (Munch Museet, Oslo), the very subject of which seems to be representative of the new manner of painting, which is helpful here in reinforcing the notion of movement. In *Self-Portrait in Orange and Lilac* (Munch Museet, Oslo), also painted in 1912, the violence of the coloring would almost lead us to regard it as a «Fauve» work, but one done in a rather Impressionist technique and in a helter-skelter mixture of colors that borders on the vulgar.

The last major works

Despite the aesthetic disorder revealed by all these works, they constitute the most spontaneous and unreflective portion of his work at this period. For Munch had now undertaken commissions for murals as well, the first of which, painted at Krageroe,

SELF-PORTRAIT BETWEEN BED AND CLOCK, 1940   Oil, 62¼″ × 50″   Collection Munch Museet, Oslo

A Bathing Establishment, 1907 Oil, 44⅛" × 35½" Private collection

WHITE NIGHT, 1901   Oil, 48⅛″ × 46″
Collection National Gallery, Oslo

WINTER LANDSCAPE NEAR KRAGEROE, 1925–31   Oil, 63″ × 56⅔″
Collection Zürcher Kunstgesellschaft, Kunsthaus, Zurich

WINTER LANDSCAPE, c. 1918   Oil, 23½" × 29"   Collection Wadsworth Atheneum, Hartford, Conn.

were for the assembly hall of the University of Oslo, where they were installed in 1916, after the artist had overcome the many difficulties involved in obtaining acceptance of them.

These large panels are in part a repetition by Munch, in a more universal form, of the ideology of his *Frieze of Life*, which, he said, had helped him to develop his «decorative sense.» The compositions bear such titles as *The Sun*, *The Human Mountain*, *The Researchers*, *History*, *Chemistry*, and *Alma Mater*. Although nothing in them warrants our viewing them as Expressionist paintings, in elaborating his themes Munch retained a spiritual attitude that may justify what the Austrian writer Hermann Bahr saw in Expressionism, namely, a manifestation of the «universal soul» (*Gesamtgeist*). The outcome of Munch's lengthy preparatory studies is very disappointing. Patient effort has succeeded violence: we feel in them a laborious studio labor in which philosophical intent does not palliate pictorial weakness.

The murals he painted in 1922 for the dining room of the Freia chocolate factory in Oslo are no better; they are a repetition, in greatly impoverished and almost caricatural fashion, of several subjects from his excellent early paintings. Even more disappointing are the paintings for the numerous panels intended for the Oslo City Hall, which he began working on in 1928 and continued until his death in 1944. It is true that in the interval, beginning in 1930, sight problems obliged him to almost completely abandon his artistic activity for several years.

During this period, however, Munch came to be considered a national hero in his native land. He wanted for neither commissions nor honors. In 1908 he was named Knight of the Royal Order of Saint Olaf, and the Grand Cross of the same Order was awarded to him in 1933. Major exhibitions were devoted to him, not only in Scandinavia but also in Cologne (1912), Zurich, Basel, and Berne (1922), Berlin and Mannheim (1927), Dresden (1929), London (1936), and Amsterdam (1937). For a long time to come, however, he continued to be unappreciated in France, and not until 1952, several years after his death, was a Munch exhibition held at the Petit Palais in Paris. Since then there has been just one exhibition of his graphic work at the Musée des Arts Décoratifs in 1969 to remind us that he was a remarkable engraver. The 1974 retrospective at the Musée National d'Art Moderne, with 86 canvases, 55 watercolors and drawings, and 116 prints can be regarded as just, if tardy, reparation for an incomprehensible omission. However, the works exhibited represent only a small portion of the 1,000 canvases, 4,400 watercolors and drawings, more than 15,000 prints, and six sculptures left by the Norwegian painter. The existence of this great body of work made it possible to establish the Munch Museum in Oslo, which was opened in 1963.

Apart from the particular features relative to the various periods of his evolution, and the aesthetic and psychological characteristics revealed by an analysis of his art, what strikes us in Munch's work (and this was probably one of the reasons it escaped the attention of many historians of modern art) is the fact that it cannot be included fully in any given «school.»

If the Expressionists adopted him, it was because his work, as embodied in a certain number of paintings, anticipated their conceptions. But, as we have seen, what Munch created goes far beyond the theoretical and formal limits of Expressionism. Thus nothing justifies the persistence with which this body of work has been classified as a

HARVESTING WOMEN, c. 1916   Mural
Festival Hall, Oslo University

90

branch of the historical line of painting, because in fact this sideline or branch is the very factor that challenges the merits of the «historical line,» and this it is, precisely, that shows Munch's independence and originality.

The fact that his output was uneven during his sixty years of creative activity is of interest to us only insofar as our curiosity about the man is concerned with the effects on his art of the contradictory aspects of his nature and the happy or unhappy events in his life. But our curiosity would be meaningless were it not motivated by the admiration aroused in us by one of the most individual and most disturbing painters of our century.

ERIK PEDERSON, 1944 Pastel on paper, 9½″ × 17⅝″ Collection The Solomon R. Guggenheim Museum, New York

BIOGRAPHY

1863. Born at Loeten, Norway, December 12.

1864. Munch family settles in Christiania.

1868. Death of his mother.

1878. Death of his sister Sophie.

1879. Commences studies at Technical Institute.

1880. First paintings.

1881. Works with Julius Middlethunt State School of Art and Handicraft.

1882. Works with Christian Krohg.

1883. Takes part for the first time in exhibitions at Modum and Christiania.

1885. Spends three weeks in Paris.

1889. First private exhibition at Christiania. Spends autumn in Paris. Works in studio of Léon Bonnat. Visits Saint Cloud. Death of his father.

1890. Spends summer at Aasgaardstrand and Christiania.

1891. Spends winter in Paris and Nice. Returns to Paris in April, staying at 49 rue Lafayette. Summer in Norway. Autumn in Copenhagen and Paris. December in Nice. Exhibitions at Christiania, Berlin, and Munich.

1892. Summer at Aasgaardstrand. Exhibition in Berlin at invitation of Association of Berlin Artists.

1893. In Berlin, moves in literary circles and meets Richard Dehmel, Julius Meier-Graefe, August Strindberg and the editors of the magazine « Pan ». Travels around Germany, taking part in various exhibitions at Breslau, Dresden, Munich, etc.

1894. First etchings.

1895. Further visit to Paris. Exhibits his works at the « Salon des Indépendants » and at the «Salon de l'art Nouveau ». Death of his brother Andreas.

1896. First colored lithographs.

1899. Visits Italy and Paris.

1902. Exhibits 22 paintings from his *Frieze of Life* in Berlin.

1903. Visits Dr. Max Linde in Lübeck and paints a frieze for his house.

1905. Exhibits at the Manés Gallery in Prague.

1906. Designs stage-set for Ibsen's « Ghosts » for the Max Reinhardt Theatre.

1907. Spends summer in Warnemünde.

1908-1909. Receives psychiatric treatment at the clinic of Dr. Jacobson in Copenhagen. Is made Knight of the Royal Order of St. Olaf.

1909. Starts work on murals for the University of Oslo.

1910. Stays at Skrubben, near Krageroe.

1912. Exhibits 32 works at Cologne.

1916. Buys an estate at Ekely, near Oslo.

1922. Paints murals for Freia chocolate factory at Oslo. Exhibits at Zurich, Basel, and Berne.

1927. Exhibits at Berlin and Mannheim.

1928. Works on decorations of Oslo Town Hall.

1929. Exhibition at Dresden.

1933. Is awarded the Grand Cross of the Order of St. Olaf.

1936. Exhibition in London.

1937. Exhibition in Stockholm and Amsterdam. Some 80 of his works are confiscated in Germany as « decadent art ».

1944. Dies at Ekely, January 23.

BIBLIOGRAPHY

1894. Stanislaw Przybyszewski, Franz Servaes, Willy Pastor, Julius Meier-Graefe. *Das Werk des Edvard Munch*. Berlin.

1902. Max Linde. *Edvard Munch und die Kunst der Zukunft*. Berlin.

1904. Emil Heilbut. *Die Sammlung Linde in Lübeck,* « Kunst und Künstler » (Berlin) n° 2, May, pp. 303-325, ill.

1905. Hermann Esswein. *Edvard Munch*. Munich and Berlin.

1917. Curt Glaser. *Edvard Munch*. Berlin.

1920. Arnulf Overland. *Edvard Munch*. Christiania.

1923. Gustav Schiefler. *Edvard Munch's graphische Kunst*. Dresden.

1932. Pola Gauguin. *Edvard Munch*. Oslo.

1933. Jens Thiis. *Edvard Munch og hans samtid*. Oslo.

1946. Rolf Stenersen. *Edvard Munch*. Oslo.

1947. Johan H. Langaard. *Edvard Munch's selvportretter*. Oslo.

1948. Ole Sarvig. *Edvard Munch's graphics*. Copenhagen.
J. P. Hodin. *Edvard Munch*. Stockholm.

1950. Sigurd Willoch. *Edvard Munch raderinger*. Oslo.

1953. Christian Gierloff. *Edvard Munch selv*. Oslo.

1955. Hans Egon Gerlach. *Edvard Munch. Sein Leben und sein Werk*. Hamburg.

1956. Arve Moen. *Edvard Munch. Seine Zeit und sein Milieu*. Oslo, 1956. Berlin, 1957.
Arve Moen. *Edvard Munch. Graphic art and paintings*. 3 vol., 1956-1958. Oslo.

1957. William S. Lieberman. *Edvard Munch, A Selection of His Prints from American Collections*. The Museum of Modern Art, New York.

1960. Otto Benesch. *Edvard Munch*. Cologne and London.
Ingrid Langaard. *Edvard Munch*. Oslo.

1961. Johan H. Langaard and Reidar Revold. *Edvard Munch fra aar til aar*. Oslo.

1962. Hugo Perls. *Warum ist Kamilla schön?* List Verlag, Munich, pp. 17-30.

1963. Eli Greve. *Edvard Munch*. Oslo.

1971. Nic. Stang. *Edvard Munch*. Oslo.

1972. Werner Timm. *Edvard Munch. Graphik.* Berlin.

1973. Gösta Svenaeus. *Edvard Munch*. 2 vol., Lund.

ILLUSTRATIONS

PHOTOGRAPHERS: Foto Cine Brunel, Lugano - G. Howald, Berne - R. Kleinhempel, Hamburg - R. E. Mates, New York - O. Vaerig, Oslo - John Webb, London - Dietrich Frh. von Werthern, Munich.